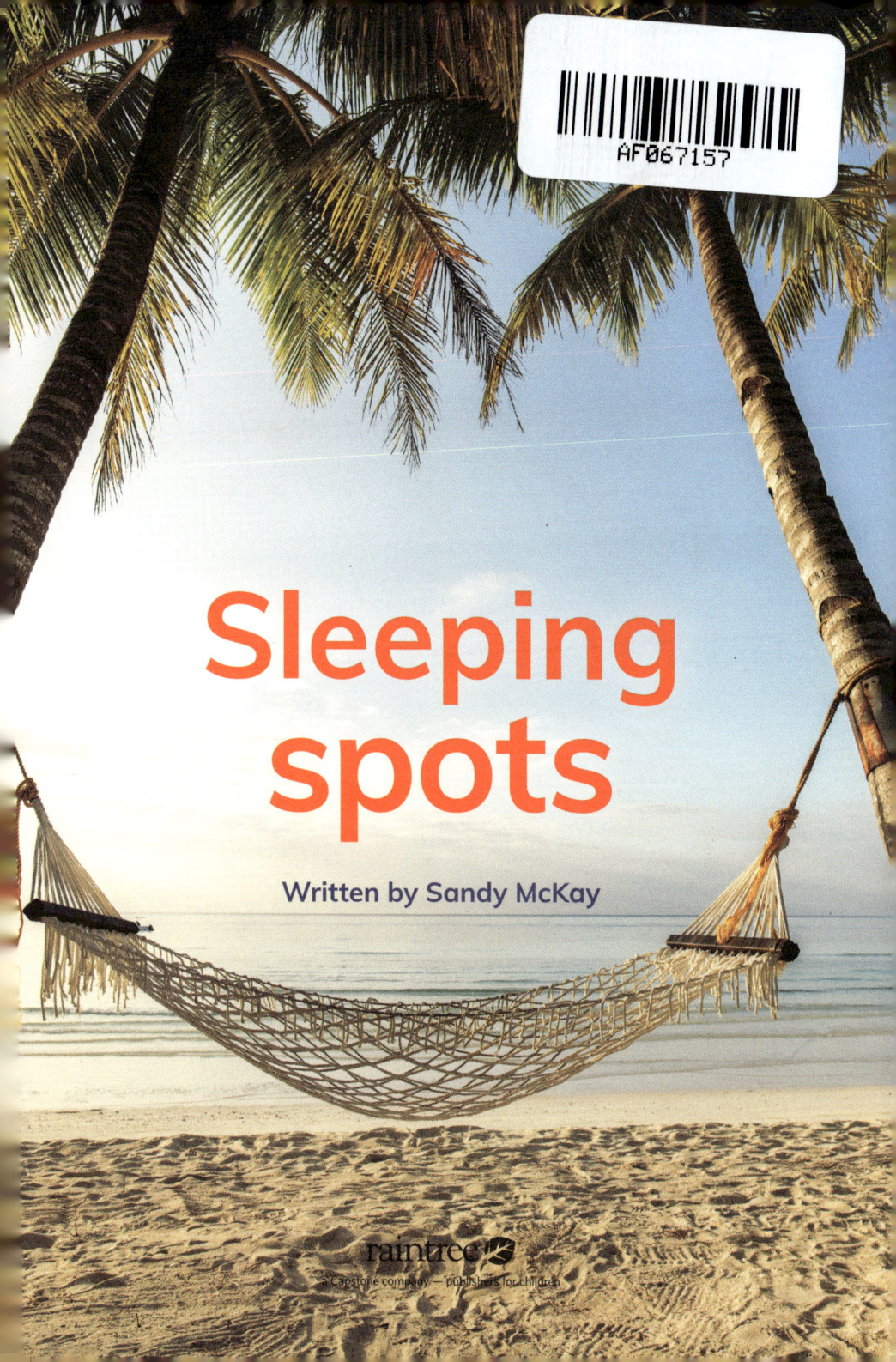

Sleeping spots

Written by Sandy McKay

Living things need to sleep, but they need the right spot to sleep in. Let's look at some good sleeping spots.

In a den

Dens might be in tree trunks or stumps or under rocks. Dens can be formed from wood or mud.

A bobcat sleeps in a den.

A fox has a den, too. A fox den might be under a shed or in tree roots.

A mum fox will sleep in the den with her little ones. But a dad fox might sleep next to the den.

Skunks, chipmunks, river otters, mink, muskrats, possums and wombats all sleep in dens.

A skunk den might be under a porch or in a log.

A chipmunk den can have lots of rooms.

A river otter's den will be on the river bank. It might be under a tree or under rocks. It might have moss in it. This den is a 'holt'.

Snug in a nest

Big storks sleep in big nests. The nests might be in trees or on roofs. Some stork nests look like they might tip off.

This nest is odd. It is formed out of spit. It can be joined to a rock or a cliff.

This is a mud nest. This is just one nest, but mud nests can be formed on top of old nests. So there can be a stack of nests up high.

This is the biggest sort of nest there is. This one is in Africa. It is lots of little nests joined up into one big nest. It is formed from twigs and sticks.

Up a tree

A tree is a good sleeping spot if you might be hunted as you nap. Tucked up high in a tree, there is less risk of ending up as dinner.

Red panda

Raccoon

Owl

Panther

Under a tree

Some hunters sleep at the bottom of a tree. No one is going to hunt them! But they do need to be out of the hot sun as they nap.

In the deep

When this one sleeps, it just rests the left part of its brain. Then it rests the right part. So all of its brain has a turn at sleeping, but it can still spot a hunter.

Cool spots for us

There are lots of cool spots for us to sleep in, as well.

A cabin in the hills

Do you like to trek? On a long trek, you might need to sleep out in the hills. A cabin is a good spot to stop at for the night. It will be in just the right spot for trekkers – not too far from town and not too near.

A cabin might not have much in it – just bunk beds in one big room. Do not forget your sleeping bag as there will be no sheets or blankets!

When you go, sweep the cabin and lock it up tight to keep the rats out.

Swinging from the trees

A hammock is a swinging bed. It might be cloth or netting. It will rock you as you sleep.

A hammock is high up, so it is a good bed if you have to sleep in the woods. There are lots of bugs and things that come out at night in the woods. You do not need them creeping into bed with you!

There is a trick to getting into a hammock. You must sit down and then swing one leg in and then the next leg. If you jump on the hammock, it will start to swing and you will be tipped out!

How to get into a hammock

How not to get into a hammock

High in the air

On a flight, you might sit in the main cabin. If so, you will have to sleep in your chair at night. Keep your belt on as there might be bumps. If you cannot sleep, you can just nap on and off. The flight attendants will bring food to you in your chair – no need to get up at all! A short flight can be fun, but a long flight will be hard if you cannot sleep.

If you are in luck, you might have a spot here. There is lots of room and the chairs turn into beds. This is good on a long flight, but it costs a lot.

On a long flight, the attendants must rest, too. There will be a spot for them to sleep in. It might be tucked at the back or up near the cockpit. It will have beds with belts for the attendants to do up when they sleep.

Glamping

You might have been camping, but have you been glamping? Glamping is camping with less effort! You might sleep in a big, big tent or in a little wooden hut. You will have a bed, not just a mattress on the mud. There will be sheets and quilts to help you sleep well.

And a hot drink might be sent right to your bed!

A summer hut

This little hut is on the sand. There is no room for a bed, but you can have a quick nap in a chair in there. It is a good spot if you need a short rest out of the hot sun.

All sorts of sleeping spots

You can sleep high up in a tree hut. That's a bit like a red panda or an owl!

Or you might curl up in an igloo. In this one, you can look up and see the stars from your bed.

Beds in a camper van? That's clever. Your bed is with you when you are on the road.

And on this big ship, you can sleep in your cabin or nod off by the pool on the ship's roof.

We all need the right spot to sleep. What is the best spot for you?